TIME
FOR KIDS
READERS

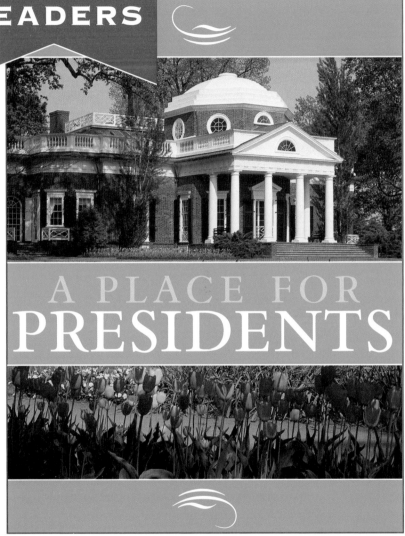

A PLACE FOR
PRESIDENTS

by Edwin Hagenstein

Harcourt

Orlando   Austin   Chicago   New York   Toronto   London   San Diego

Visit *The Learning Site!*
www.harcourtschool.com

The United States is a big country, and every part of our country is different. Its people also have many differences. That's because our ancestors came here from every part of the world.

Although we have differences, we are one people. The one individual who most represents this idea is the President of the United States. The President is voted on by all the people and is the one person who represents all of us.

The United States really needed to be brought together in its first years. The country had a person who could do the job. As a general, George Washington led the American troops in the Revolutionary War. He was our first President. George Washington earned his nickname, "the Father of Our Country."

Before he was the Father of Our Country, Washington was a son of Virginia. He was born in Westmoreland County, Virginia, in 1732 and grew up on his father's farm in Fredericksburg. When George was 11 years old, his father died. He stayed on the farm for five more years, studying math and land surveying. Then he moved to Mount Vernon to live with his older half-brother, Lawrence.

At Mount Vernon, George worked at surveying other people's land. When Lawrence died in 1752, George took over Mount Vernon. He now owned valuable land in Virginia and West Virginia.

George Washington loved his home, but he was often called away from Mount Vernon. In 1753, Washington volunteered to join the army. Washington returned to Mount Vernon in 1758 and married Martha Dandridge Custis in 1759. When the colonies began to fight for their independence from Britain, Washington was named commander in chief of the Continental Army. He led American troops in the Revolutionary War.

Because he had been a good leader during the war, people wanted Washington to lead the nation after the war. For his presidential inauguration in 1789, Washington once more left Mount Vernon. This time he was traveling to the nation's new capital, New York City. Leaving Mount Vernon made him unhappy. He said he was going north, "with a mind oppressed with more anxious and painful sensations than I have words to express."

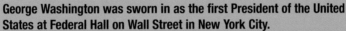

George Washington was sworn in as the first President of the United States at Federal Hall on Wall Street in New York City.

Washington had good reason to feel nervous. The United States had not been a nation for long. He knew that the country was deeply divided. Many Americans were more loyal to their states than to the new federal government.

There were other problems, too. Everyone had different ideas about what the new government should be like. No matter what steps the new President might take, he was sure to anger someone.

When Washington started his job, things went from bad to worse. Two of his best advisers opposed each other and often disagreed. Newspapers attacked Washington and others in the government. But he was a strong leader. He did not take the side of any one political group. Washington did what he thought was best for the nation.

Washington believed that no other leader could hold the country together. So, he agreed to serve two full terms as President. By the end of his second term, Washington realized that the United States had survived its difficult start. Thanks to his leadership, the nation was stronger. When asked to serve a third term, he refused. Instead, Washington decided to live out his life at Mount Vernon. In 1799 he died and was buried there.

George Washington was the first, but not the last, Virginian to be elected President of the United States. Four of the first five Presidents were from the Old Dominion, as Virginia is nicknamed.

This painting shows George Washington (right) meeting with a representative from France (left) at Mount Vernon.

Thomas Jefferson was the next Virginian elected President of the United States. He was the nation's third President, after Washington and John Adams. Born in Albemarle County, Virginia, in 1743, Jefferson graduated from the College of William and Mary. He was very talented. He could do many things, from playing the violin to reading Greek and Latin. He even designed his home, Monticello (mahn•teh•SEH•loh).

Before he was elected President, Jefferson had a lot of political experience. In 1776 he helped write the Declaration of Independence, explaining why the colonies wanted to break away from Britain. Jefferson was elected governor of Virginia in 1779. After the Revolutionary War, he served as secretary of state under George Washington. Jefferson was also Vice President under John Adams.

By the time Jefferson became President of the United States in 1801, the government was much stronger. It had the respect of the nation's citizens. It was even beginning to impress European countries.

At the time, some people thought the federal government should have

Thomas Jefferson was the chief writer of the Declaration of Independence when he was 33 years old.

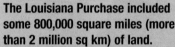

The Louisiana Purchase included some 800,000 square miles (more than 2 million sq km) of land.

believed that power should stay in the hands of the people. He tried to bring common touches to his office. He often held small, private dinners at the White House for friends and visitors.

Jefferson wanted to make the life of the common person better. One way he did this was to open western lands for Americans wanting to start a new life. In 1803 he bought the territory of Louisiana from France.

The Louisiana Territory was a very large area of land between the Mississippi River and the Rocky Mountains. Over the years, Louisiana and 12 other states were created from the Territory. The Louisiana Purchase made the United States almost twice as big. This was one of Jefferson's greatest gifts to the United States.

Like George Washington, Thomas Jefferson missed Virginia while serving as President in Washington, D.C. He called the job of President "splendid misery." Jefferson loved the countryside of Virginia more than any other place. "These mountains are the Eden of the United States," he said. He died at Monticello on July, 4, 1826.

James Madison, Jefferson's close friend, loved the hills of Virginia, too. Madison was born in 1751 in Port Conway, Virginia. He attended the College of New Jersey (known today as Princeton University). He became an expert in history, law, and government. Madison returned to Virginia and helped write the state's constitution. From 1780 to 1783, he was a delegate from Virginia to the Second Continental Congress.

For the next three years, Madison served as a member of the Virginia House of Delegates. He tried without success to get the state to approve a public school system and to gradually end slavery.

Madison also supported the idea of a Constitution for the United States. Before the creation of the Constitution, the states were only loosely connected. Instead of working together, they argued with one another. James Madison thought that Americans needed a strong national government to bring the states together. As he read about the history of other nations, he looked for examples of good and bad governments. He wanted to know what worked best and what didn't work. At the Constitutional Convention of 1787 he used these ideas to help shape the writing of the Constitution. Because of this, Madison is sometimes called the "Father of the Constitution."

James Madison was able not only to help write the Constitution but also to help make it work.

In 1789 Madison was a member of the first House of Representatives and as a member of Congress, Madison helped write the Bill of Rights. These first 10 amendments, or additions, to the Constitution state the rights and freedoms of the people of the United States.

During much of his life, Madison was closely connected with Thomas Jefferson. Madison became Jefferson's secretary of state in 1801, serving until 1809. In 1808 Madison was elected President of the United States. Like Washington and Jefferson, Madison served two terms in office. He was President from 1809 to 1817.

Madison faced challenges during his term as President. The United States fought the War of 1812 against Britain. During the war, the British captured the nation's capital, Washington, D.C., and set fire to the White House.

But the nation survived. By 1816 the United States was growing stronger every year. Still Madison was eager to return to Virginia. In 1817 he returned and he lived there until his death in 1836.

This painting shows United States and British forces battling each other during the War of 1812.

Another Virginian, James Monroe, was elected President in 1816. He was the fourth Virginian to serve as President. Following George Washington's example Monroe served two terms as President.

James Monroe was born in 1758 in Westmoreland County, Virginia. The years before the start of the American Revolution were exciting times to be young in Virginia. As he grew up, Monroe was surrounded by talk of freedom and independence.

By the time he entered the College of William and Mary, Monroe knew he wanted to fight against British rule. So he joined the Continental Army at the age of 17. He fought alongside George Washington. Monroe was there when Washington crossed the Delaware River to attack the British in 1776. While fighting at Trenton, New Jersey, young Monroe was wounded. He recovered in time to join Washington again in 1777. Together, they survived the terrible winter at Valley Forge, Pennsylvania.

James Monroe never lost the spirit of those times. He always believed in the right of people to be free. After he became President, he continued to fight for freedom.

James Monroe served as the U.S. Minister to France from 1794 to 1796.

At the time, South Americans were engaged in a similar fight. They struggled against the rule of European nations. As a growing power, the United States tried to help. Monroe set forth the Monroe Doctrine. It declared that the United States was willing to go to war to stop European nations from expanding their empires on the American continents.

James Monroe retired from the presidency in 1825. The leaders of his time had formed a new nation. They had helped the United States through its difficult early years.

TFK
DID YOU KNOW

Would you like to visit the homes of Presidents from Virginia? Here is where they lived.

MOUNT VERNON: George Washington's home overlooks the Potomac River in northern Virginia. It is 15 miles (24 km) south of Washington, D.C.

MONTICELLO: The home of Thomas Jefferson is outside of Charlottesville, Virginia. Jefferson designed his home and much of its plantation.

MONTPELIER: James Madison's plantation and home in Orange County, Virginia, is famous for its views of the Blue Ridge Mountains.

ASH LAWN–HIGHLAND: James Monroe's friend Thomas Jefferson helped design this Charlottesville plantation. Monroe loved his home here and called it his "cabin-castle."

BERKELEY PLANTATION: William Henry Harrison grew up on this plantation in Charles City County, Virginia. The beautiful mansion includes the room where Harrison was born.

SHERWOOD FOREST PLANTATION: John Tyler bought this plantation in Charles City County, Virginia, while he was President. He named it Sherwood Forest referring to his reputation as a political outlaw.

MONTEBELLO: The name of Zachary Taylor's birthplace means "lovely mountain." It is near Gordonsville, in Orange County, Virginia.

THE WOODROW WILSON BIRTHPLACE: Visitors to Wilson's birthplace in Staunton, Virginia, can look at his family's household belongings and learn about Wilson's public life.

William Henry Harrison

John Tyler

The next two Virginians to serve as President are often thought of as a pair. William Henry Harrison and John Tyler were both from Charles City County, Virginia. In 1840 Harrison was elected President, and Tyler became Vice President. Their run for the Presidency was a wild one. It used advertising, speeches, and songs designed to capture people's attention.

William Henry Harrison was born in 1773, just a few years before the fight for independence began. By the time he was a young man, the United States was growing. The nation was young and energetic. Young Harrison, like many others, looked to the West to make his mark in the world. The West was where the nation was moving.

As it happened, Harrison did earn a name for himself on the frontier. He gained the nickname Tippecanoe while serving as the governor of the Indiana Territory. In 1811 Harrison led his men in battle against the great Shawnee leader, Tecumseh. The fight took place close to Tippecanoe River. Harrison's victory there made him famous.

Harrison's term as President was shorter than that of any other President. Soon after his inauguration speech, he became ill. Before he had been in office a month, William Henry Harrison died.

John Tyler took over as President and served out the term. He was born in 1790 in the Tidewater region of Virginia. He knew a great many of the leading figures in Virginia politics.

William Henry Harrison was the first President to die while in office.

The most important contribution Tyler made happened soon after he became President. Because Tyler had not been elected President, his advisors wanted him to share power. The advisors said that Tyler should form a team to govern the nation.

Tyler disagreed. "I can never consent to being dictated to," he answered. "I am the President . . . When you think otherwise, your resignations will be accepted." Tyler set an example for later Vice Presidents. Afterward, when a President died in office people looked to the Vice President to lead the nation.

Tyler was stubborn. He wanted everyone to agree with him. This did not make him a popular politician, and he made many political enemies. He was not reelected President.

This almanac cover was an advertisement for the election of William Henry Harrison and John Tyler in 1840.

Just four years after John Tyler's presidency, another Virginian was elected. President Zachary Taylor was from Orange County, Virginia. He was born in 1784. Zachary Taylor and James Madison were second cousins, but they were not much alike. Madison loved education and the comfortable life of a Virginia planter. Zachary Taylor was more restless and sought adventure. As a young man he headed West, joined the army, and fought on the frontier. Taylor rose steadily through the army's ranks during the early 1800s. In time, he became a general.

Zachary Taylor was born in Virginia but grew up in Kentucky.

By 1846 he was a United States military leader in the Mexican War. During that war he led his troops into the thick of the fighting. They called him "Old Rough and Ready." His victories made Zachary Taylor famous across the United States. His fame helped lead to his election as President.

Taylor was elected President in 1848. He did not serve out his term. On July 9, 1850, he died of food poisoning.

Taylor's brief time in office was filled with problems. The most serious was the possibility of a civil war. The nation was arguing about the issue of slavery. Some Southern states wanted to separate from the rest of the Union. Zachary Taylor stood firm. He said the nation must remain together.

It was 63 years before another Virginian served as President. Woodrow Wilson was the son of a minister. He was born in 1856 and lived in Staunton as a young boy. Little Tommy, as he was called in his childhood, spent many Sundays in church where he heard his father's sermons.

Wilson was much like his father. He became a great public speaker. He was a scholar, too. More than anything, Woodrow Wilson wanted to change the world. He wanted to make it a better place.

Before entering politics, Wilson was most interested in education. When he attended the College of New Jersey (today known as Princeton University), Wilson enjoyed debating and studying history. Before graduating in 1879, he read all he could about history. Wilson went on to teach history in college. He became the president of a university (Princeton University) long before he became President of a nation (United States).

Woodrow Wilson

After doing so well in education, Wilson decided to enter politics. He believed it was a way he could make a difference in people's lives.

The *Lusitania* had sailed peacefully many times before being attacked and sunk in 1915.

Wilson took the office of President of the United States in 1913. In 1914 World War I began in Europe. Wilson worked hard to keep the United States out of the war. Then, in 1915, a German submarine sank a passenger ship, the *Lusitania*. More than 1,000 people died, including 128 Americans. The attack was one of the reasons the United States later entered the war in 1917.

The fighting in World War I was brutal. The deaths and the destruction that resulted saddened President Wilson. Still, he hoped that its end would mean an end to wars for all time. World War I was called the "war to end all wars."

Wilson spoke out about the values of the United States. He said that all nations had a right to decide their own futures. He called for an international force to protect small nations. Above all, he called for a group of nations to settle international arguments. Talking over problems in a calm way was better than war, he believed. For his work, Woodrow Wilson won the 1919 Nobel Peace Prize.

Nearly 90 years have passed since a Virginian was elected President. Even so, no other state has produced more national leaders. They guided the United States through difficult times. Leaders such as Washington, Jefferson, Madison, and Wilson were proud Virginians whose dedication, loyalty, and wisdom helped protect the nation's freedom and make our nation strong.

DID YOU KNOW

Some states that were homes of Presidents.

STATE	NUMBER OF PRESIDENTS
Virginia	8
Ohio	7
Massachusetts	4
New York	4
North Carolina	2
Texas	2
Vermont	2